Dedication

To Dan & Mike

Thank you
For giving
Me someone
To call
When I am
Lost and Worried
Of getting caught
In a coming Storm.

Cans Of Worms

selected poems

Michael Robert Neal

Made with ❤ on the BookLeaf Publishing Platform
www.bookleafpub.in
www.bookleafpub.com

Preface

I never sought out to become a poet. Before the global
pandemic, I was teaching yoga at good job, planning
more future workshops, starting my own and new
classes. And then the fitness industry tanked. I moved
back home to my hometown of Canton, Ohio, having a
couple different jobs, trying to get back on me feet.

Something in me broke during the course of the last few
years. Whatever it was that broke inside me unleashed a
whole host of angry, sad, hostile, vicious emotions.
Despite my best efforts and attempts I've had my fair
share of struggles to get it together, having falling outs
because I couldn't bring myself to care anymore.

The poetry started on its own. I graduated in 2019 from
college with philosophy degree and had a habit of
posting self-help thoughtful quotes I synthesized from all
the reading I did. The idea was that maybe the progress
of my own journey could help others. It didn't seem like
anyone cared or noticed. They definitely noticed the
occasional fitness pictures, but the random thought
bubbles not so much.

Since no one cared much about what I did or what I was

talking about (so it seemed) the thought bubbles turned into poetry. Very raw very emotionally laden vulnerable poetry. (I never had even read much poetry). I read mostly non-fiction work, like self-help books, books on philosophy, culture, history, science, etc. I don't know where the poetry came from, why poetry and not fiction like I did when I was younger, and why I never had decided to publish a book until now.

I never cared much about the poetry. It was a relief, a relaxing habit; something I typed up and threw away. Sure it got me a small following on social media, but I never cared about what happened to it. This book is an attempt to rectify that. Opening up a whole host of raw and vulnerable emotions. Comfortable or not.

In this book are some of my favorites, some of the works that still resonate with me, and some poems I can recite word for word without thinking about it. They aren't much, but I hope you enjoy.

Michael Robert Neal

Acknowledgements

Thank you to everyone who helped make this book possible. Thank you especially to my house mates Daniel Schmier and Michael Bryant for being there with me through some of the hardest periods of growth I've ever had to face in my life. Thank you also to my social media audience for keeping me going. It's nice to know someone has been watching and reading.

I have too many sources of inspiration and gratitude to thank, so thank you. I hope this book shows my feelings in all their honesty to those I am grateful for and to those whom I thank everyday for the blessings I have been lucky enough to have received.

1. my tea

Should I have spun
my tea
Just to watch it swirl
and vortex
Should I have beat
the leaves
I steeped and brewed?

2. It takes a couple eggs

It takes a couple eggs
To make an omelette
But the issue is that
It takes a couple dollars
To buy the eggs and
The eggs might be broken
Before you even opened
Up the carton. Maybe one
Was cracked on the bottom
Hidden from plain sight
Maybe it cracked on the
Way home from the market
When you hit that bump
In the road. Maybe you
Just dropped one as you
Went to make your breakfast
It takes a couple of eggs
To make an omelette
It takes even more than
That to make a good one
It takes dedication learning
Practice and Skill and Luck
To make a good one. Maybe
It needed some seasoning

Maybe your pans suck
And you can never get the
Eggs not to stick or you're
Not using enough butter
Or oil or margarine. Maybe
Your spatula is cheap and
Ineffective at rolling up
The eggs up from off the pan
It takes a couple of eggs
To make an omelette
It takes even more than that
To make one worth eating
And make one you'd want
To try and make again or
Feel confident enough to
Serve to other people without
Getting upset or anxious
Or scared about it. You know
How easy it is to make a
Bad omelette? It takes more
Than just a couple eggs
It takes Time and Practice
And Skill and Luck. It takes
A couple of omelettes to
Even make one you feel
Proud enough to make you
Eat your Own. Let alone

Want to use a couple more
Eggs to make another one
Without giving up half-way
Through and making a scramble
Instead. It takes a lot to make
An omelette as it turns out.
It takes a lot more than just
A couple of eggs. First and
Foremost it takes a Kitchen
And Chef and Market where
You can buy them. It takes a
Fridge. It takes a will and a way
To make them without making
Yourself insane over what
Was just supposed to be a
Nice breakfast. It takes a lot
To make a good omelette as it
Turns out. At least without making
You scramble your own brains
Instead. It takes a lot sometimes.
And that's ok to admit. Sometimes
Everyone deserves to make a big deal
Over a couple of cracked eggs on the stove
It's why we had omelettes for breakfast
And not just quick and easy scrambled eggs
It takes a big deal to make an omelette
It takes effort and focus and concentration

It takes making a bigger deal over the eggs
To make an omelette so yes
It takes a lot sometimes, and yes
You and your breakfast can be made
A big deal over. Just don't forget
To cry over the milk that morning
After you spill it as you make
Your way to the table, as you cracked
Your couple of eggs over that
Big deal you made in the kitchen
It took a lot more than just a couple of eggs
To make that omelette, didn't it?
I bet you got stressed out at some point
Along the Way.

3. Brownie

We grew up with
This little Shih Tzu
Named Brownie
He was white
And with some
Patches of Brunette
I think he deserved
A better home than ours
I think he's in a better
Place now. But he came
Last night to visit me
In my dreams and
I remember all those time
He went out of his way
To take a shih tzu in my room
My room was upstairs
And was no where where
He needed to be
My older sister was always
Upset her play room was gone
Maybe he only went up there
When he was mad or maybe
I did something wrong
But then I think about

How that dog was sometimes
The only other boy in the house
And how those dogs
Were bred for Emperors
How they symbolize good luck
We certainly weren't a royal lineage
And that dog did not live in a palace
Full of Harmony
At least he lived in Canton
At 314 on 36th st in a red brick house
With a green roof, behind a big park
Right in our backyard
I think we all learn
That we're all bad people
Who deserve bad things
To happen to us as we get older
To help us explain why they happen
In our minds, but Brownie
Was a dog bred for Emperors
And he cuddled me whenever
I was sick or after I had surgery
He didn't like me all that much I think
I think I got so distracted trying
To get away from all the fighting
I got so angry at myself for
Getting angry. I don't like
causing trouble for other people.

It seems like
They'll use whatever they can
As an excuse to get upset
over nothing these days.
Even when you try
to be thoughtful or do the right thing.
I don't think I'm a good
nor a bad person. I think
I'm a person who's
Been someone lucky enough to
Have someone go out of their way
To shih tzu in their room
to make sure I think of him
long after he's gone.
So I think I want
To be a good luck charm
Someone and something that
Makes it easier to get up
Out of bed and to fall asleep
And dream. Something and someone
That makes life worth bearing with
Someone who helps people get better
Because it's suddenly the path
Of least resistance even if it's
Out of the Way.

4. people are allowed to lie to me

People are allowed to lie
To me for I do not know
The full nor the whole
Truth anyways people

Are allowed to lie to me
For I do not know every
Nor all of the truths of
The any and every world

Anyways people are allowed
To lie to me for I do not know
Everything that came before

The moment in which they
Did nor do I know their full
Nor true intentions and reasoning

Behind it people are allowed to lie
To me for I have lied to other people
For big reasons and for small I am

Sure people are allowed to lie to me

For sometimes lying simply means
I am afraid of getting and being hurt

Once more people are allowed to lie
To me for sometimes lying looks like
Santa Claus people are allowed to

Lie to me for sometimes the truths
We thought we knew and held dear
Turn out to be false and or useless

People are allowed to lie to me for
Sometimes it is safer to do so rather
Than be hurt or killed or punished

Unjustly people are allowed to lie
To me for if there is no truly good
Virtue nor no truly evil Vice then
Honesty is not fully good nor Lying

Fully evil. People are allowed to lie
To me for I know the truth is not
Always easy to swallow nor bear
In every and any moment people

Are allowed to lie to me for I know
That I am not always right and people

Are allowed to be wrong people are
Allowed to lie to me for fiction is

Something that is fun and that is
Useful people are allowed to lie to
Me for I know the word tree is not

A tree people are allowed to lie to
Me for everyone is making it up as
They go along and everyone is
Taking their best guess, putting
Their best foot forward as they
Make their way stumbling around
In the dark big ambiguous world

People are allowed to lie to me for
I know I have survived both the
Truth of the world as it's deceits.
I can do so again if I choose and
Need be.

5. from the Heavens

I do not expect anything from the heavens
because the heavens do not expect anything from me
and as I walk through their tears today
I know they cry them just so that they may tell me
how hard all of this was on them
Perhaps the burden of the heavens
is the heaviest of all to bear
but that does not change the fact
that today I must walk to work in the rain
because the heavens are burdened by my presence
perhaps they are disappointed in me
perhaps they are shamed
they expect me to be warm in the hell they have
regulated me to
thinking that would be enough of a gift
to get through the world
that looks at me with a sneer and in disgust

6. the event

be the event
they didn't know
they should have
bought tickets to.

7. make a snow angel

Make a snow angel
While you shovel the snow
To remind yourself
That work can be made
Light of and Fun often
Takes hard work to
Even be had. Give yourself
The grace to be made a
Fool of and look silly
As you mumble and shout
About how much you
Hate the cold and how
Long the driveway is
That brings you such
Pride to take photos of
And show off to other people
Remind yourself it's not
That hard to be a kid again:
You just forgot how to be
Among all those things
Taking up space in your head
As you learned how to be
An adult with all those
Important things to do

And books to read and
Places to go. Trust fall
Yourself into the snow
And shake it all about
As if people didn't wish
All the time they could
Go back to being a kid
Again. Well looky there:
The opportunity was right
There in the snow right next
To your whining you brought up
With the shovel.

8. Today I Laughed

Today I Laughed
The best laugh I ever laughed.
It was all because of me.

The joke was set up
So far in advance—
Even I forgot.

But here it came,
Back around to greet me.
To brighten my day,
To lighten my body.
The sun rose within me.

Here I am,
Writing its poem,
With words that
Could only wish
To do it justice.

I think I made myself laugh—
Truly, for the first time ever.
And the joke was mine,
Crafted so far in advance.

I'm sure there are
Only more to come,
For they have

Only just begun.

9. Do Something Stupid

Do something stupid
Something that makes no sense
Not a lick
Something that has no logic behind it
Other than to make something dumb happen

Life is short
Life is unpredictable
Life is cruel and inhumane for no reason
So be as unpredictable as Life

Do something stupid
Just to make it happen and say you did it
And have fun doing it too
Just for shits and giggles

It's the thing that helps the Sun
Come out of the dark cave of Night
Hiding from all the anxieties and offenses
Of the World

10. I Became the Crazy Thing

I became the crazy thing—
I didn't know what else to do.
I read my books.
I worked hard at my job.
I tried to be with family and friends.
I asked for help when I could.
I always asked for feedback.

I don't even drink, never have.
Never smoked a cigarette in my life.
I'm always eating healthy,
Working out when I can.

I followed what felt good and right.
I pushed myself into discomfort,
Put myself out there,
Tried new things—
But still, I became the crazy thing.

I didn't know what else to do.

Now I wonder if I should have—
Yelled, screamed, cried,

Taken it out on others
Instead of letting it slide,
Letting it go.

But that wouldn't've helped anyone,
Least of all me.

Man, I fucking hate that pandemic.
It fucking ruined everything.
I'm so fucking mad at it.

Powerless against a world-altering event,
It changed everyone and everything.

Sometimes, you just go crazy.
I'm sure everyone did—
Even if just a little bit.

11. Meditation

Meditation
Is learning
How to do
Nothing

Meditation
Is learning
To let life
Pass one

By and
Accept
Reality
As it is

Be it with;
Silence
And or
With noise

Meditation
Is sitting
And standing

Meditation
Is let
Nothing
Happen more

Than anything
Else at all
And letting
Nothing
Change things

More than
Anything one
Can actually do

Meditation
Is like
Sleeping awake

And isn't
Sleeping
And dreaming

One of
The most useful
Things one can
Do but not do?

For isn't one
Doing nothing
More than
Anything else
While sleeping?

For sleeping
And dreaming
Happen on
Their own

It is something
Demanded
Of us

Something that
Can and does
And will happen

When and as
It needs to

Isn't it funny
How some of
The best things
One can do

For oneself
Is absolutely
Nothing at all?

Oh how
Important it is
That one learn
How to do
Nothing

More than anything
Else in order
To free oneself
From one's own
Karma. For even

Yoga is only
Preparation
For the work
Of doing nothing
That is Meditation.

12. Repeat After the Poem

Repeat after the poem:

When I disrespect and abuse my body
I disrespect and abuse
The people who have helped me
Love and care for it.

When I disrespect and abuse my body
I disrespect and abuse
The people who have helped me
Learn to love and care for myself.

When I disrespect and abuse my body
I disrespect and abuse
The people who love and
Care about me.

Learning to respect and care
For oneself, one's body,
Mind, and spirit
Is learning to respect, love, and care

For those who respect, love,
And care about us.

13. sometimes the spinach spoils

Sometimes the spinach
you spent money on
will rot and mold and waste.
It was an option,
not an ultimatum.
Don't cry over
spoiled spinach.
There will always be
some things
That go to waste
and spoil.

14. oh why, oh sky

Oh why, oh sky
why can the clouds
not come to dim
the moon,
that I must learn
to sleep beneath
with such a bright

15. Fear is a Common Thing

Fear is common
Like the rain

Fear is common
Like the sunshine behind

The clouds
Fear is common

Like the starshine and
The moon

Fear is common
Like the night and
The day

Fear is common
Like the eclipses of
The bodies in the skies

Fear is common
Like the silence and
The noise

Fear is common
For it lurks everywhere

Fear is common
For it can appear
At any time

Fear is common
Meaning it can be
Dealt with as if
Routine and as if
Mundane.

Fear is common
So do not worry if
It comes your way
For fear is a common thing

Things never seem to change
Much around here
The horse farm two doors down
And across the street
Started off with one horse here
When I arrived one year prior
Now they have six
Did I really look away for that long?
I remember being excited
When they got two
I've yet to even meet the first
Let alone their owners
I've been here for more than year now
They say things are always changing
I guess that happens at it's own pace
A pace I seem to struggle to keep up with
Those horses are still gazing the field
Just as it was when there was only one
Now there's six
I wonder how much has changed
I don't even know why they raise horses
Maybe they like the company
Every one needs someone at some time
Or another

17. Poor has Never Meant 'Good'

Rich does not
Mean evil for
Poor has never
Meant Good

Wealth does
Not mean Evil
For Poverty
Has always
Meant Bad
And Awful

Wealth is a
Fact of Life

There has
Always been
People with
More or Less
Than one Another

The Value of
Wealth and

Currency itself
Fluctuates

Over and Over
And Over again
It has no
Inherent value

For everyone
Knows money
Gets more or
Less depending
On the time
And place.

Money belongs
To no one
It simply gathers
Where and when
It goes. Money

Comes and Goes
And it's worth
Comes and Goes
Just as much

Even the rich

Go broke and
Gamble as if
They were making
It up as they go
Along. Money

Is learning how
To take and spend
Risks. The poor
Simply cannot
Afford them

While the rich
Can afford to
Risk other people
In the process

18. The river

The river
Was not
even
A river

When I
Thought I
I had
Stepped in
It once

The river
Was not
Even a
River

The river
Was a
Stream

A flow
An ocean
Waiting
To pond

As if
It were
A lake

When did
The puddle
Become a
Rushing
From the
Rains?

When did
Flood
Turn the
Continents
Into islands

A top
A ball
Of blue?

19. Kindness is not always 'nice'

I wanted to do
The wrong thing
Because I got
Tired of trying
To do the good
And feel like
I was and am
Going no where

For it. And here's
The thing: being
Nice is not the
Same thing as
Being kind, for
Kindness is not
Always nice.

Sometimes
You have to
Stand up to
Both yourself
And other people

And call them
Out for being
An asshole

Or being crazy
And have a fight

Sometimes you
Have to walk out

Sometimes you
Have to go crazy

Because the
Alternative is to
Bear more weight
On your shoulders
Than you can bear

Kindness is doing
The hard work of
Standing up both
To and for yourself

20. everyone hates their money

I think everyone hates their money
At one point or another. They hate
How much of it they have. They hate
How little they seem to make. They
Hate that they have to spend and save
It they hate that they have to budget
They hate that it's something everyone
Else wants from them they hate that
It's something they want from others
For themselves they hate that they
Always seem to have to have it and
Do something with it or that they
Never seem to have the right amount
To cure all their ills and ailments.
Money keeps on talking like it never
Shuts up: all it wants to do is chatter
And chatter and chatter about nothing
At all it seems: who to give it to, how
Much of it to give and how often,
Money seems to be a reckless toy
People made to play a game called
"Productivity" it makes us feel good
To spend it makes us feel bad to spend

It makes us want things and then it
Makes us hate ourselves. It's never
Doing enough. It never gets us enough
It's never ever enough. One day it
Might be worthless and now there's
This new type of money that's nothing
But numbers on a screen and suddenly
The paper in your wallet needs to be
A microchip in a phone or a computer
Or a tablet. And suddenly you're not
Smart enough anymore and suddenly
All you do is move it around like how
You take boxes and bags of food out of
Boxes and bags only to put them into
Other boxes and bags so other people
Can put them into boxes and bags
At the grocery store. Here's a bunch of
Numbers: I have enough numbers
In a bank on a screen and they tell me
I can have these other things. Of that's
The case why are we not just giving
People numbers to start with? If that's
What they need to play the games
Both people with lots of money have
And people with no money have
Like how people do nothing but play
And make and design games for a living

Why are people not just given a bunch
Of numbers to start with? Like how
Monopoly starts you out? Is that game
Just about spending and making and
Taking and passing around the money
So other people can try and make
And take and spend and pass around
Money? Some people make it off of
Food. Some people make it off of Sex.
Some people make it off of books.
Writing. Jewelry. Art. There's an
Endless amount of ways to make
Money. All they need is money to make
It with. Some people just talk. Some
People make the chairs and tables
And microphones for those people to
Talk with. I think hate my money:
It always seems like no matter what
I do I'm not making enough sound
Choices with it. Even though I'm told
I need to eat good food. Have good
Sleep and clothes and get out of
The house and do things with other
People. I'm so tired of trying to do
Anything anymore it always seems
Like it's the wrong choice. The only
Choice it seems like it sometimes

Is to starve and do nothing. What am
I supposed to do when there are just
Things that make me feel better or
Make me feel happy? Not pursue them?
Deny myself every little thing? What
About experiences? What about
Investing in oneself? Money is
Supposed to grant one freedom until
You realize you have to cater to
Whatever it wants and the whims
Of whomever has it and whom you
Have to make it off of or from. Or else.
I wish money would shut up. All it's
Good for is gossip and talking itself
To death.

21. makes messes

You're allowed to make messes
And leave them for later

You're allowed to make messes
And learn to clean them up

You're allowed to make messes
For fun and for art and pleasure

You're allowed to make messes
Just to have something to clean up

You're allowed to make messes
And figure out how to clean them best

You're allowed to make messes
You cannot clean up by yourself

You're allowed to make messes
That lose things or help other things
Be found.

You're allowed to make messes
In order to reorganize your mess

Into something else.

You're allowed to make a mess
Into a new one. Ultimately that is
What it is and will become.

What is a party if not a mess waiting
To happen? What is a mess if not
The proof of a life being lived?

What is a mess if not the aftermath
Of activity and work and play?

Some messes are simply the way
A reserve or a surplus is stored

Having messes to deal with is
How businesses start how solutions
Are made and bought and sold

Having messes is what gives one
Something to do and goals to pursue
Or simply avoid.

How many messes
are made and unmade simply to
Avoid making and unmaking another?

How many messes are the mess
Left behind by another or made
To hide the others?

How many messes
Are just decorations that have
Been made to look nice and give
Scenery and structure to the house?

How many messes are simply
Art pieces on the wall to distract
From an empty barren wall one was
Upset had no mess?

What messes
Do you want to have?

What messes
Do you want to be able to make and
Undo?

What messes do you want to
Organize and tidy and clean?

What messes do you want to have to wear
Or house or use to decorate?

What is a salad if not a mess of leaves?
What is a forest if not a mess of trees?
What is an ocean if not a mess of water?
What is dog or cat if not a mess of fur?

What is a person if not a mess bound
Up together in messes larger and
Greater than itself whether or not
It made them itself?

www.ingramcontent.com/pod-product-compliance
Lightning Source LLC
LaVergne TN
LVHW041239200726
843507LV00013B/2741